Transcribed by David Pearl

ISBN 1-57560-626-7

Visit our website at www.cherrylane.com

CONTENTS

The Yu-Gi-Oh! Story

Meet Yugi and his best buds, Joey, Tristan and Téa. They share a love for the newest game that's sweeping the nation: Duel Monsters!

Duel Monsters is a card-battling game in which players pit different mystical creatures against one another in creative and strategic duels! Packed with awesome monsters and mighty spell-cards, Yugi and his friends are totally obsessed with the game.

But there's more to this card game than meets the eye!

Legend has it that five thousand years ago, ancient Egyptian Pharaohs used to play a magical game very similar to Duel Monsters. This ancient game involved magical ceremonies, which were used to foresee the future and ultimately, decide one's destiny. They called it the Shadow Game. Since the game used so many magical spells and ferocious creatures, it wasn't long before the game got out of hand and threatened to destroy the world. Fortunately, a brave Pharaoh stepped in and averted this cataclysm.

Now, in present times, the game has been revived in the form of playing cards.

Meanwhile, Yugi's grandfather gives him an old Egyptian puzzle that no one can solve, but when Yugi finally pieces the puzzle together, his life is forever changed. The puzzle instills Yugi with an ancient spirit, and the two working together form a stronger, more confident duelist.

Soon after, the mysterious creator of the Duel Monsters card game, Maximillion Pegasus, kidnaps Yugi's grandfather and Yugi is drawn into a Duel Monster's competition that Pegasus arranged. Now Yugi must duel his way through a tournament and defeat Pegasus in order to save his grandfather.

How will Yugi do it? Will the help of his friends, his belief in the heart of the cards, and the mysterious power of his magical Millennium Puzzle be enough?

Giant monsters! Powerful magic! And ancient Egyptian legends! It's your move.

Yu-Gi-Oh! Theme

Words and Music by
John Siegler and Wayne Sharpe

Your

Time 2 Duel
(Frog Jam)

Words and Music by
Russell Velazquez

I'm Back

Words and Music by
John Siegler, John Loeffler
and Norman Grossfeld

Moderately fast

Instrumental...

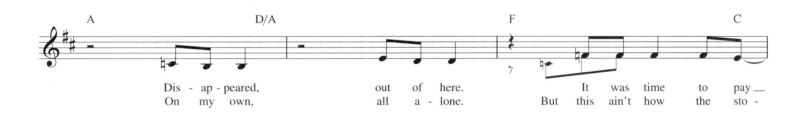

Dis - ap - peared, out of here. It was time to pay
On my own, all a - lone. But this ain't how the sto -

___ my dues. ___ Nev - er guessed that you'd be dressed
ry ends. ___ Now I see those close to me.

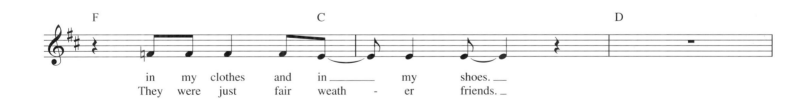

in my clothes and in ___ my shoes. ___
They were just fair weath - er friends. ___

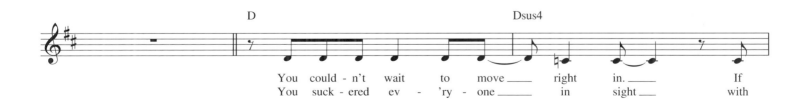

You could - n't wait to move ___ right in. ___ If
You suck - ered ev - 'ry - one ___ in sight ___ with

Your Move

Words and Music by
John Siegler, John Loeffler
and Norman Grossfeld

Duel Madness

Words and Music by
Joel Douek

Moderately fast

(Spoken:) Virtual systems ready! Instrumental...

(Spoken:) Got - ta find a way, just to play, just a lit - tle game. Got - ta com - pul - sion, wan - na be a cham - pion!

Got - ta feel the heart, got - ta be smart, play the card. Got - ta get in - side the mind of my coun - ter - part!

Instrumental...

(Spoken:) That's the key, _ I'm a split per - son - al - i - ty. A duel sen - sa - tion, that's my des - tin - y! _

I've got duel ____ mad - ness in my brain! _ Mon - ster in -

flu - ence ____ in my veins! _ (Spoken:) Got - ta find a way in - side this fan - ta - sy,

Hol - o - graph - ic duel - ing mon - ster re - al - i - ty. Got - ta find a way, got - ta see my strat - e - gy. I'm

No Matter What

Words and Music by
Lloyd Goldfine and John Siegler

Ahead of the Game

Words and Music by
Michael Whalen

Moderately

Instrumental...

Not so fast; you think you've won. __
I cre - ate the games we play. __

I'm here to say we're far from done. __
Ev - 'ry de - tail is mine to say. __
Just you wait and
You have luck; you

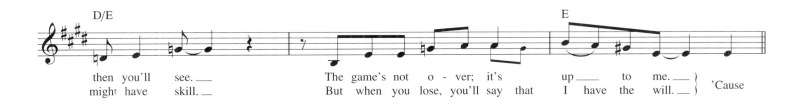

then you'll see. __
might have skill. __
The game's not o - ver; it's
But when you lose, you'll say that
up __ to me. __ }
I have the will. __ }
'Cause

I am __ a - head of __ the game, __ and

noth - ing __ will be __ the same. __

All my tech - nol - o - gy, all my smarts, my cre - a - tiv - i - ty will

rip you _ a - part. My liq - uid - i - ty, my gi - ant bal - ance sheet, _

all my se - crets. Hey, *(Spoken:) I don't e - ven cheat.* 'Cause I am ___ a -

head of ___ the game when we're stand - ing face _ to face ___ and noth - ing ___ will

Repeat and fade

be _____ the same; when I put you in ___ your place. _ 'Cause

We'll Be There

Words and Music by
John Siegler and Julian Schwartz

Slowly

Instrumental...

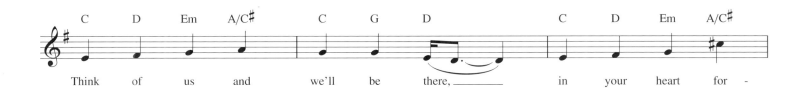

Think of us and we'll be there, _____ in your heart for -

ev - er. Some - times ___ when you're un - sure, _____

some - times ___ when you're a - fraid, ___ at times it's hard to

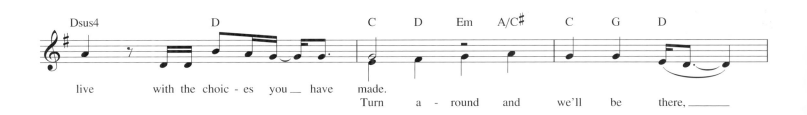

live with the choic - es you ___ have made.
Turn a - round and we'll be there, _____

al - ways by your side. _____ When it's time to stand the test, _____

I know you'll shine a - bove the rest. ___ When you try and find your

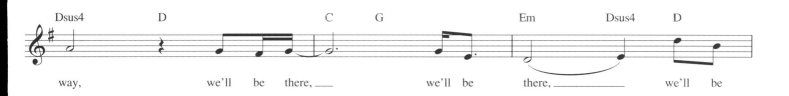

way, we'll be there, ___ we'll be there, ___ we'll be

there, ___ we'll be there. ___

To Coda ⊕

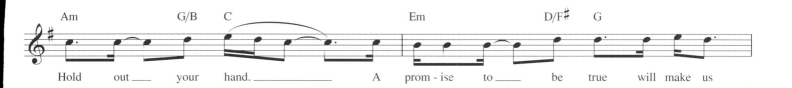

Hold out ___ your hand. ___ A prom - ise to ___ be true will make us

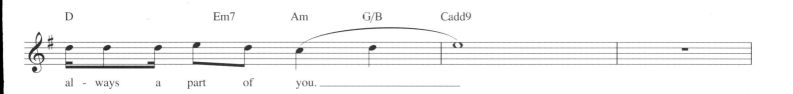

al - ways a part of you. ___

D.S. al Coda

Instrumental...

Coda ⊕

We'll stick to - geth - er through thick and thin. _ That's the mean - ing of a real ___ friend. _

Repeat and fade

And when it's time to stand _ the test, _ friend - ship shines a - bove _ the rest. ___

Face Up Face Down

Words and Music by
Wayne Sharpe and Louis Cortelezzi

Instrumental...

Wel - come all my hon - ored guests to the ul - ti - mate duel with the best of the best.
Is - n't it grand what I've man - aged to do, by kid - nap - ping those clos - est to you.
What's wrong now? You look so sad. Los - ing your soul does - n't feel that bad.

At my in - vi - ta - tion you've come to com - pete _____ for the
I've tak - en their souls to lay on the line _____ in a
Those you love have told me so, _____ and

hon - or of suf - fer - ing the fi - nal de - feat. _____
win - ner take all
soon, my friends, you

Instrumental...

duel for all time. _____ Let's play the game. _ I'm
too will know. _____

sure you all _ know how. _ But watch your - selves, _ my fool - ish friends. You're all in my _ world _ now. _____

Heart of the Cards

Words and Music by
Eric Stuart and Questar Walsh

Moderately

Instrumental...

Long a - go in an - cient times, a sa - cred game was played of both spir - it and mind.
There's a pres - ence deep with - in. Search your soul, take con - trol, you will win.

Sev - en i - tems hold the mys - ter - y: Puz - zle, eye, neck - lace, ring, rod, scale, and key.
Two forc - es in - ter - twined. Just need the guid - ance of an o - pen mind.

Who will make the fi - nal stand? Make the move; the an - swer lies in your hand.
There's a pow'r that's all a - round. It de - scends from the friends who won't let you down.

And wheth - er you win or lose hangs in the bal - ance with each card you choose.
And when you come un - done, they stand by your side till the duel is won.

Trust. Trust in the heart. _ Don't let down your guard. _ The heart of the

To Coda

cards. No bat - tle's too hard. Re - mem - ber to trust in the heart of the

cards.
Yu - Gi - Oh! Yu - Gi - Oh!

(Spoken:) Time to duel. Instrumental...

D.S. al Coda

Coda

*cards.
Yu - Gi - Oh! Yu - Gi - Oh!

Sing 1st time only

1. 2. 3.

(Spoken:) Time to duel.

Trust in the heart of the cards.

World of Yu-Gi-Oh!

Words and Music by
Russell Velazquez

Moderately fast

Instrumental...

Yu - gi Mu - tou, where R U? The Phar - aoh's call - in' me. I will at -
Max - i - mil - lion Peg - a - sus, don't put that eye on me.

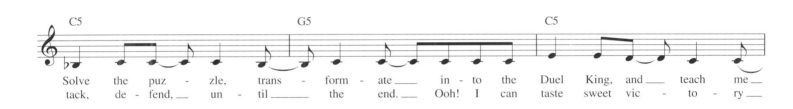

Solve the puz - zle, trans - form - ate in - to the Duel King, and teach me
tack, de - fend, un - til the end. Ooh! I can taste sweet vic - to - ry

(like Ya - ma Yu - Gi), sum - mon - ing and de - fend - ing.
(like Ya - ma Yu - Gi). Yo! Peg - a - sus, can U read my mind?

Face down flip ef - fect. Fu - sion is the vi - tal key. Ex - o - di - a, the For -
If you can, tell me what you find. It's time 2 duel, Mai dar - ling

bid - den One. I - I - I - It's in my pos - ses - sion now, the D - D - D - D - Duel is done!
Val - en - tine. And tell her that the art of duel - ing I will re - de - fine.

More Great Piano/Vocal Books
from Cherry Lane

For a complete listing of Cherry Lane titles available,
including contents listings, please visit our web site at
www.cherrylane.com